LET'S MAKE HISTO

The Dark Ages

Paul Titley

Illustrations by Ken Petts
Models and diagrams by Hilary Evans

OWLET BOOKS
London·Sydney·Toronto

A BYZANTINE BALANCE

Constantinople, the capital of the Byzantine Empire, was a flourishing city. Merchants came from Europe and Asia to trade in its markets and shops. The city government kept a close check on this trade. It controlled prices so that customers could not be overcharged, and sent officials to shops to inspect the accuracy of the balances used to weigh goods.

Byzantine traders were proud of their balances, which were not only accurate, but also very beautiful. They were usually made of iron and bronze, an alloy of copper and tin. The pans were hung on delicate chains suspended from elaborate hooks. The metal weights that slid along the balance lever were cut into attractive shapes. A particularly popular design was a woman's head and shoulders.

How to make the balance

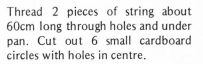

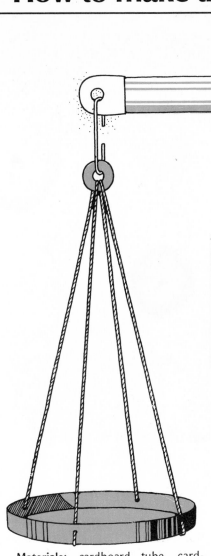

Thread 2 pieces of string about 60cm long through holes and under pan. Cut out 6 small cardboard circles with holes in centre.

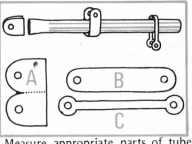

Measure appropriate parts of tube and cut 3 cardboard shapes A, B, C. Glue A over flat end of tube. Glue B onto tube near flat end. To enable C to slide along balance lever, glue only circular parts.

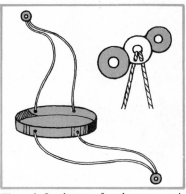

Thread 2 pieces of string on each side through cardboard circle. Loop strings over and glue in place. Glue cardboard circles to each side as shown to form strong loop. Hang pan from paper clip hook at flat end of balance lever.

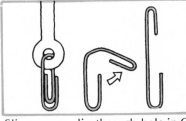

Slip a paper clip through hole in C. Straighten 2 paper clips and hook them through holes in A and B.

Materials: cardboard tube, cardboard, 3 paper clips, string, circular cheese box, modelling clay, scissors, pencil, glue, paint, paintbrush

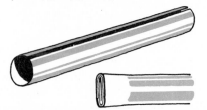

Cut down length of cardboard tube. Roll it up tightly and glue along cut edge. This will be balance lever. Flatten one end of tube.

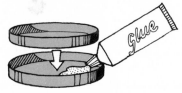

To make the pan, glue circular box lid into its base. Make 4 equally spaced holes in the side.

Model a piece of clay into head of a woman, or other shape. Press paper clip hanging from C into top of clay. Paint balance with brown or metallic paint.

BYZANTINE JEWELLERY

Byzantine jewellery is among the most beautiful the world has ever seen. The craftsmen worked in small workshops with simple tools. There was a small furnace and a pair of bellows in the corner of the workshop. Leather pouches hung from the edges of the wooden workbench to catch any scraps of precious metal. The metal was beaten out with hammers on a small anvil. Sometimes it was held in a vice and cut with a variety of small tools that looked like chisels. Patterns and designs were tapped into the metal with punches.

Byzantine jewellers used both gold and silver. They were extremely skilful in heating gold and drawing it into thin strands of wire that could be worked into intricate designs called filigrees. Pearls, emeralds, and amethysts brought from India were set into the gold and silver ornaments.

How to make the jewellery

Materials: cardboard, egg box, ring openers, string lentils, split peas, macaroni, clay, paints, paintbrush, scissors, glue, ballpoint pen, sticky tape, safety pin, Indian ink, newspaper, silver foil

Cross and chain: Cut out a cardboard cross 12 × 10 cm. Glue on ring openers as mounts for jewels. The jewels can be beads, buttons or rounded tops of egg boxes.

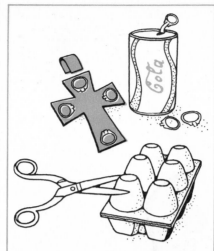

Glue lentils and split peas round edges. Make a cardboard loop. Glue it at top of cross. Paint cross and decorations gold. Colour jewels if necessary.

The long beads are macaroni pieces painted gold. The round ones are made from clay. Thread beads and cross onto string.

Brooch: Place a 16 cm square of foil (shiny side down) on a pad of newspaper. Using a tin or cup to form the circle, draw brooch pattern with a ballpoint pen.

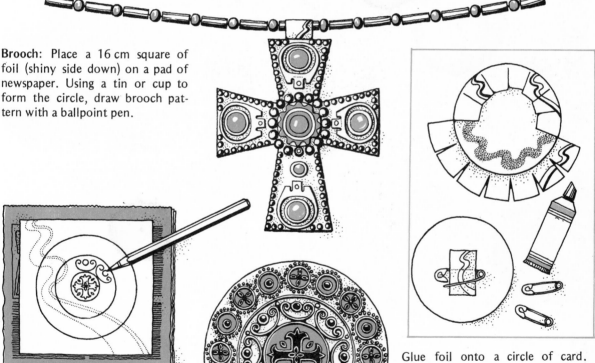

Paint shiny side of foil with Indian ink. When it is dry, carefully wipe ink from raised pattern with a damp cloth.

Glue foil onto a circle of card. Cover back with another circle of card. Tape a safety pin onto back. Colour some of the patterned areas.

BYZANTINE FORK AND SPOON

The Byzantine craftsmen used the same skill with which they made jewellery to produce very beautiful forks and spoons. These were made of silver mixed with copper to harden the precious metal. The designs were extremely elaborate. The handles were made by taking a rectangular bar of silver, cutting notches into it at measured points, and then slowly twisting the metal round and round.

As far as is known there were no knives to match the spoons and forks. The Byzantines used their daggers to cut meat.

Forks were not in use at all in western Europe at this time. They seem to have been introduced to Europe from Byzantium by Italian merchants.

How to make the fork and spoon

Materials: silver foil, wire, drinking straws, twine, silver paint, paintbrush, glue, scissors

Spoon: Bend piece of wire 44 cm long in half. Form bowl and twist handle pieces together.

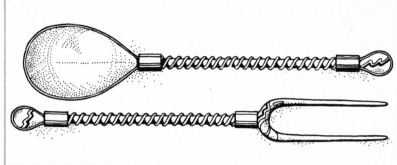

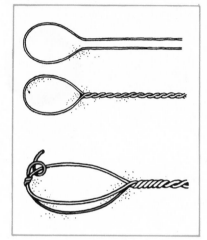

Join a wire from handle to top of bowl.

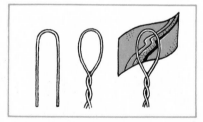

Bend an 11 cm length of wire in half. Twist ends together. This forms end for the handle.

Glue strips of foil over bowl and handle end piece.

Cut a straw just longer than the twisted wire handle. Glue handle and handle end piece into straw.

Wind some twine diagonally around the straw. Glue ends.

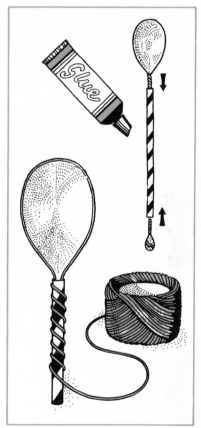

Paint straw and twine silver.

Wind and glue foil strips at both ends of the straw.

Fork: Make a T shape from two 22 cm lengths of wire. Twist the handle pieces together. Glue strips of foil around bar of the T.

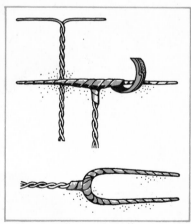

Make the middle section thicker by winding on more strips.

Bend the prongs into shape. Make the fork handle in the same way as the spoon.

7

VIKING LONGSHIPS

In longships like these Vikings from Norway, Sweden and Denmark raided the coasts of western Europe. A typical Viking ship was 24 metres long and built of oak. The huge keel was carved by axe from a single tree. The framework of 19 ribs was placed on the keel. The ribs were not fixed rigidly to the keel, so that in rough seas the body of the ship could move slightly, and stood less chance of being pounded to pieces.

On each side of the ribs were 16 rows of planks, called strakes, overlapping one another. Each strake was rivetted to the one below with iron nails. The ribs were lashed to lugs on the strakes with fir roots and whalebone. The

strakes were caulked with tarred animal hair to make the ship completely waterproof.

The ship carried one sail about 5 metres square. The mast was mounted on a large block of wood set along the keel, and was fixed firmly with an oak wedge. It could be lowered quickly by removing the wedge.

There were 16 pairs of oars. Movable flaps dropped over the oarholes in the strakes when the oars were drawn in. An early form of rudder was mounted at the rear of the ship on the righthand side.

How to make the longship

Materials: cardboard, paper, string, 2 wooden dowels 38 cm and 28 cm, a cotton reel, scissors, modelling knife, glue, paint, paintbrush

Divide cardboard into 4 cm squares. Draw shapes and cut them out. Make holes for oars and mast.

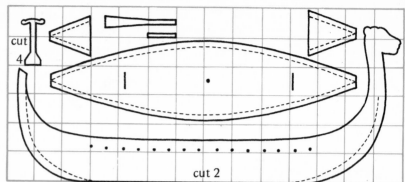

cut 4

cut 2

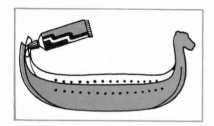

Score dotted lines on ship's sides. Glue sides together at prow and stern. Glue a narrow cardboard strip around the neck.

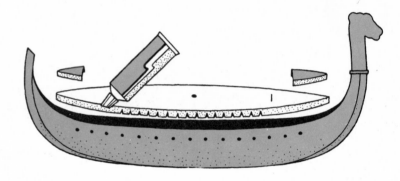

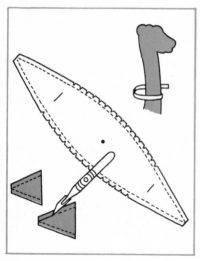

Score floor section and two strengthening pieces. Cut away notches at curved edges. Fold edges over and glue floor section into the ship. Glue the strengthening pieces at each end above floor.

do not glue this section

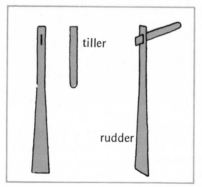

tiller

rudder

Score T-shaped mast rests and glue each pair together. Push them into slits in floor, fold back edges and glue down.

Glue tiller into rudder. Glue rudder to stern on the outside.

Paint ship, including mast rests and rudder. Paint in figurehead.

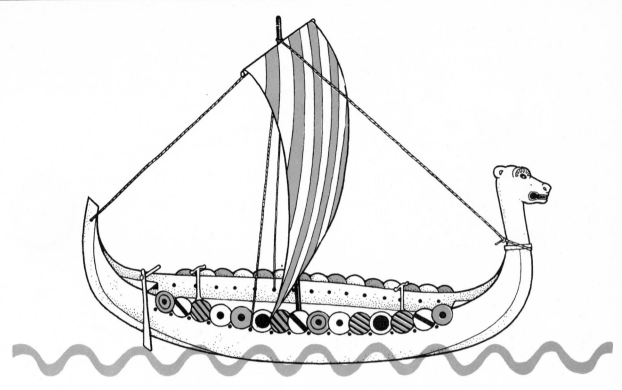

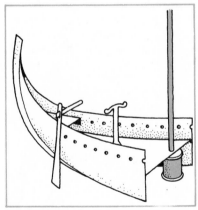

Glue cotton reel under ship's floor. Fix mast into cotton reel.

Bind crosspiece (yard) onto top of mast. Cut 26 cm square paper sail. Paint diagonal strips across it and glue it onto yard.

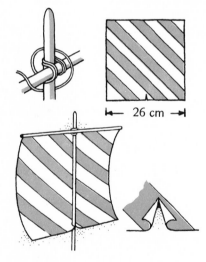

← 26 cm →

Make slit in sail. Bend sail upwards and glue it onto mast. Secure with sticky tape if necessary.

Tie string rigging from mast to oar holes at the ship's sides, and from mast to tail and neck.

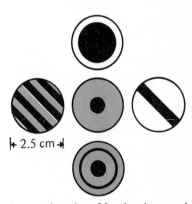

← 2.5 cm →

Cut and paint 30 circular cardboard shields. Glue them between oarholes on ship's sides.

A HUN BOW

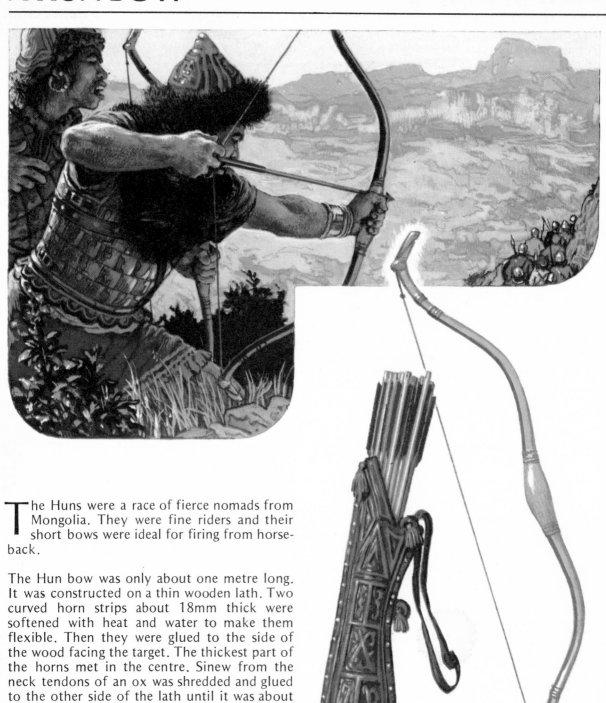

The Huns were a race of fierce nomads from Mongolia. They were fine riders and their short bows were ideal for firing from horseback.

The Hun bow was only about one metre long. It was constructed on a thin wooden lath. Two curved horn strips about 18mm thick were softened with heat and water to make them flexible. Then they were glued to the side of the wood facing the target. The thickest part of the horns met in the centre. Sinew from the neck tendons of an ox was shredded and glued to the other side of the lath until it was about 5mm thick. Notches to hold the bowstring were cut into the wood at each end. The bowstring was made from plaited animal hair or skeins of twisted silk. A strong man could fire an arrow at least 300 metres with such a bow.

How to make the bow

Materials: metal coat hanger, cardboard, newspaper, modelling clay, string, canes, glue, wallpaper paste, paint, paintbrush, scissors, pliers

Cut handle from a metal coat hanger—use pliers or keep bending wire until it snaps. Ask an adult to help. Bend wire into bow shape.

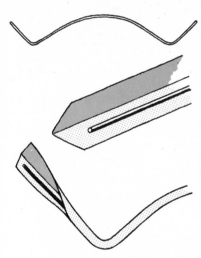

Fold strip of cardboard 4cm wide in half. Glue wire inside, extending card beyond wire at each end. Glue on another strip covering edges of first one.

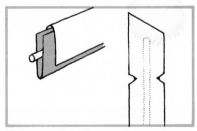

Trim ends diagonally and cut notches for bow string.

From large sheet of newspaper cut 2 strips 7cm wide and 1 strip 5cm wide. Paste paper with wallpaper paste. At one end of each length make a 1.5cm fold and keep folding.

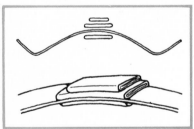

Paste longer folds of newspaper on either side of bow Paste small fold on top of outer long fold.

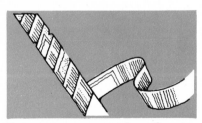

Cut some narrow strips of newspaper. Paste them and wind them around bow. Add another layer of pasted strips.

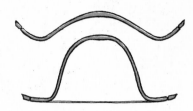

Before newspaper covering dries, string the bow. Leave it to dry thoroughly.

Paint bow with emulsion or poster paint, and varnish.

Make arrows from pieces of cane, dowel or sticks. Point one end and weight with clay. Notch other end.

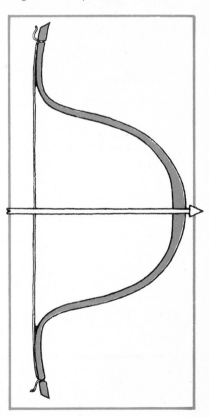

DRINKING HORNS

Beautifully decorated drinking horns have been found all over Europe. They were usually made from the horns of cattle or oxen, although the Saxons in Germany used the huge horns from the now extinct bull-like animal called an aurouch.

Drinking horns were decorated in a variety of ways. Most often, silversmiths hammered out leaves of silver, decorated and lacquered them to look like gold, and pressed them onto the rim of the horn. Then they forced bands of silver-gilt up the horn until they fitted firmly. They decorated the tip of the horn with a silver-gilt animal's or bird's head.

In Sicily carved ivory drinking horns have been found, probably made from the tusks of young elephants. They are believed to have been the work of Muslim craftsmen.

How to make the drinking horn

Materials: 1 large and 2 medium size plastic cartons, paper, newspaper, thin card, kitchen foil, glue, scissors, wallpaper paste, sticky tape, pencil, paint, paintbrush.

Cut down sides of 2 medium cartons. Remove rims and bases. Open cartons out flat. Trim away sides as shown.

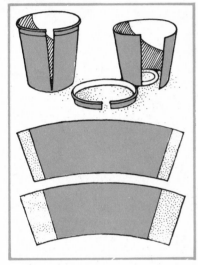

Rejoin sides of cartons with sticky tape. One carton will be a bit larger than the other. These two cartons form the middle section of the horn.

Take the large carton and fit the 3 sections together. Keep the joins on the underside of the horn.

Bend the 2 middle sections upwards and fix in place with sticky tape.

Make a paper cone 1½ times the height of smaller carton for last section of horn.

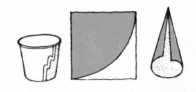

Fix cone on horn with sticky tape.

Using wallpaper paste, stick small pieces of newspaper over horn. When newspaper is dry, paint horn.

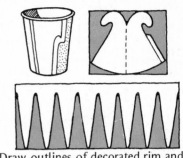

Draw outlines of decorated rim and tip of horn on thin card. Cut out.

Place shapes on shiny side of piece of kitchen foil and draw round them with soft pencil. Remove shapes and draw in patterns.

Glue card shapes onto decorated foil and cut round them. Form the tip and glue over end of horn. Glue scalloped piece around rim.

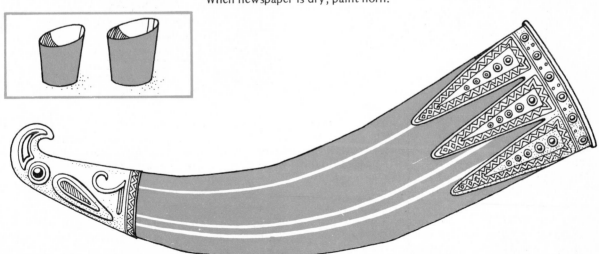

A SAXON HELMET

A number of different types of Saxon helmets have been discovered. The type of helmet most commonly worn by the Saxon warriors is shown in this picture. The frame was made of strips of iron, and filled in with pieces of leather or horn. Some helmets had a crest of a bird or animal on the top. Some also had pieces of metal projecting over the forehead or extending down to protect the wearer's nose.

Helmets like these could withstand glancing blows from swords, but offered no protection against heavy battle axes that could be wielded with great force.

How to make the helmet

Materials: cardboard, crêpe paper, rubber band, scissors, pencil, ruler, glue

Cut strip of cardboard 4cm wide and long enough to fit round your head. Glue ends together to form a band.

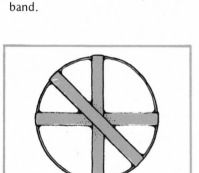

Cut 3 strips of cardboard 2cm wide for helmet dome. Glue them to inside of headband.

Cut 1 strip of cardboard 4cm wide and 4 cm longer than 3 narrow strips. Round one end. Glue strip to inside back of headband, over top of narrow strips, and to front of headband.

The long rounded end is nose guard.

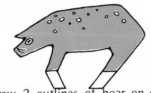

Draw 2 outlines of boar on cardboard and cut out shapes. Glue 2 boars together except for tabs on feet.

Bend tabs outwards and glue boar to top of helmet.

For lining, cut sheet of crêpe paper same length as headband. Glue edges together. Gather one end and secure with rubber band. Turn inside out and glue into helmet. Cut away excess paper.

ANGLO~SAXON LYRE

Very little is known about music in the Dark Ages, but the remains of lyres like the one in the picture have been found. It was a wooden instrument about 70 centimetres long, 16 centimetres wide, and 2 centimetres deep. It had six strings made of animal sinew. They stretched from the wooden tuning pegs at the top, over a small bridge, down to the base of the sounding board. This lyre was decorated with two plaques representing birds' heads.

The performer plucked the strings with his fingers. Only very simple tunes could be played on an instrument like this. Lyres were mainly used by Saxon poets just to accompany their songs and poems. There is no evidence of minstrels or bands of professional musicians travelling from town to town in the Dark Ages.

One lyre was found in a warrior's grave in Germany, which suggests that men would often play and sing to amuse themselves or their friends around the campfires.

How to make the lyre

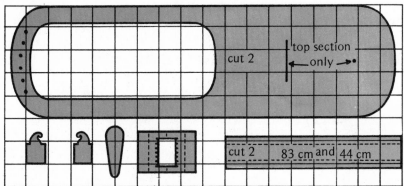

cut 2

top section only

cut 2   83 cm and 44 cm

Paint the small piece of cardboard. Glue it at end of lyre just covering strings.

Paint decorative pieces gold. Draw the pattern and colour the jewels. Glue decorations onto lyre.

Materials: cardboard, matches, nylon thread, paints, black ink, glue, scissors, paintbrush, craft knife, pencil, ruler

Divide cardboard into 2cm squares. Draw shapes and cut them out. Cut slit and string hole in top section.

Score edging strips. Cut out notches where strips curve at rounded ends of body section.

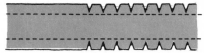

Glue strips onto top section of lyre. Fix small inner strip first.

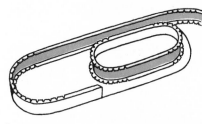

Score bridge section. Fold in half and glue as shown. Cut 6 notches for strings. Push bridge through slit in top section, and glue in place.

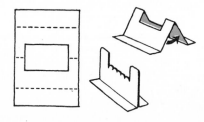

Cut six 45cm lengths of nylon thread. Knot together and thread through hole in top section.

Glue bottom section in place. Paint the lyre and draw in some wood grain lines.

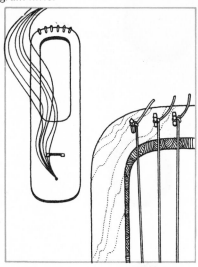

Sharpen 6 used matches and cut notches at top. Push them through holes in lyre. Take strings over bridge and tightly knot each string round a matchstick.

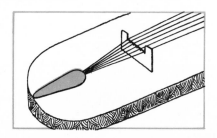

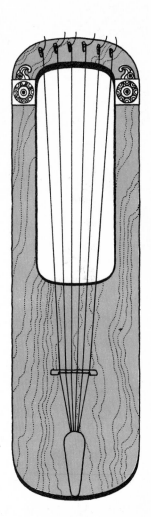

THE FRANKISH STIRRUP

One of the most important inventions of the Dark Ages was a little device all horse riders now take for granted, the stirrup. The use of stirrups meant that armed knights could sit much more securely on their horses than before. They could charge with their lances and slash with their swords without constant fear of being unhorsed. The use of stirrups made the Frankish knights into the most effective fighting men of the Dark Ages.

No one knows exactly when stirrups were invented, but their shape differs little from those used today. Wealthy knights took great pride in the appearance of their horses. After blacksmiths had hammered out the iron stirrup, they were often asked to engrave patterns in the metal. Some knights even took their stirrups to silversmiths to have them plated with silver.

How to make the stirrup

Materials: thick cardboard, cardboard, ice cream stick, gummed paper strip, string, ruler, pencil, scissors, glue, paint, paintbrush

Cut strip of thick cardboard 2 x 30cm. Crease cardboard 4.5cm from ends. Carefully bend strip into stirrup shape and secure with gummed paper strip.

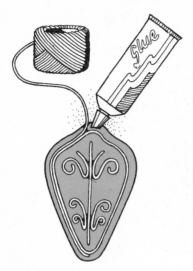

Glue string on side pieces to form the decoration.

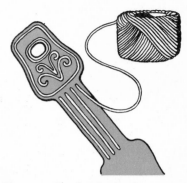

Glue on string for decoration.

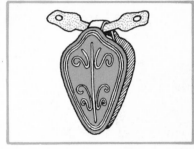

Slip this piece through loop at top of stirrup and glue in place. Paint stirrup silver.

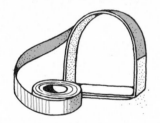

Cut ice cream stick to 9cm. Glue it under stirrup. Cover entire stirrup with gummed paper strip.

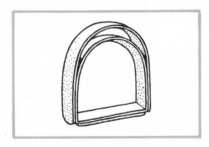

Cut strip of thick cardboard 2 x 24cm. Round ends and carefully bend into shape. Glue to stirrup so that it forms a loop at top. Glue side pieces to stirrup.

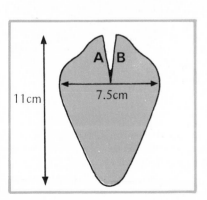

Cut 2 cardboard side pieces. Use gummed paper strip to join edges A and B on inside.

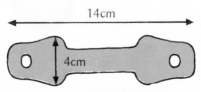

From cardboard cut out piece to join stirrup to strap.

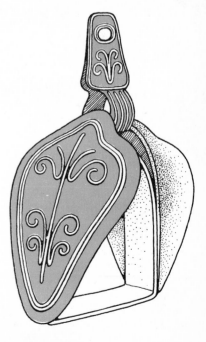

THE FRANKISH SWORD

The invention of the stirrup enabled Frankish knights to fight on horseback with longer swords than before. The Frankish sword was about one metre long, broad-bladed and double-edged, and had a rounded point. It was made by forging and welding several rods of iron into a solid block and, while the metal was still red-hot, introducing carbon into it to make a form of steel. The head of the blade was hammered to a thick point, and then passed through the guard, inside the grip, and secured by the pommel.

Kings' and nobles' sword guards and hilts were often magnificently decorated with red enamel, gold and plate, and precious gems. The scabbards were usually made of rivetted leather and always decorated. Some were even made of solid silver.

How to make the sword

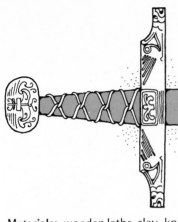

Materials: wooden laths, clay, knife, string, cardboard, glue, scissors, pencil, paint, paintbrush

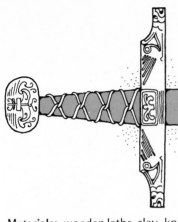

Round the end of a wooden lath 60 x 3.5cm. Shape handle as shown.

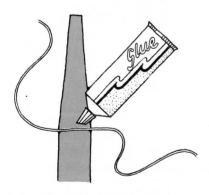

Glue a length of string to base of shaped handle.

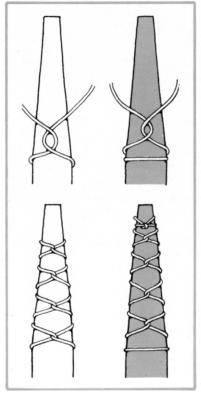

Loop string diagonally around handle. Knot ends and glue them to handle. Dab some glue where strings loop together.

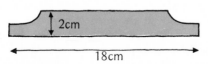

Cut another lath 18 x 2cm for guard. Shape top edge.

Place guard on piece of cardboard. Draw round guard and cut out cardboard shape. Glue wooden guard to blade. Glue cardboard guard to wooden one from other side of blade, enclosing blade.

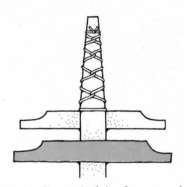

Form a flat oval of clay for pommel. Press it onto handle end. When clay pommel is dry, paint sword.

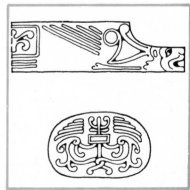

Paint decorative patterns on guard, handle and pommel.

LOMBARD BROOCHES

During the Dark Ages wealthy men and women wore beautiful brooches and clasps to ornament or secure cloaks and gowns. The brooches were made in a wide variety of designs and patterns. Some were of pure gold, others of solid silver. Many were richly inlaid with garnets, turquoise and pearls. Sometimes these stones were mixed with glass paste jewels to add to the variety of colour.

Many attractive brooches and clasps had a background of red enamel patterned with delicate gold filigree work. This gold thread was made by covering fine silver wire with gold leaf and heating it over a charcoal fire. Although this kind of jewellery was made in many parts of Europe, the most beautiful was produced by the craftsmen of Lombardy.

How to make the brooch

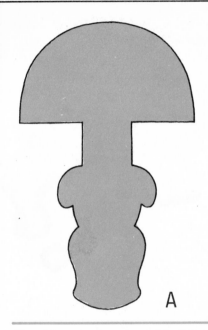

A

B

C

Materials: cardboard, gold foil, matchstick, cottonwool, safety pin, beads, pencil, glue, scissors, pen, Indian ink, sticky tape

Draw shapes A, B, C on cardboard. Cut them out. Glue B pieces onto A. Glue C pieces on top of brooch shape.

Spread glue thinly over brooch shape. Cover with gold foil. Carefully press foil into contours formed by layers of cardboard, using matchstick tipped with cottonwool. Trim foil. Fold edges over and glue to back.

Draw in decorations with black Indian ink. Glue on jewels: use beads, buttons, balls of foil paper, or coloured cake decoration balls.

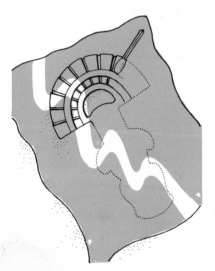

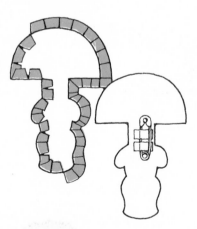

Cut another cardboard shape A and glue over folded edges. Fix safety pin to back of brooch with sticky tape.

A PLOUGH

The original plough used in the Middle East and Mediterranean countries had only a wooden spike, which could cut into light soils, but was useless on clay. During the Dark Ages a more advanced plough that could be used on all soils was gradually developed.

The coulter sliced the soil vertically with its cutting edge. The share was triangular and made a horizontal cut beneath the furrow slice.

The mouldboard turned over the furrow slice so that the ground was drained as well as being dug.

These parts of the plough were usually made of wood plated with iron. The main beam, to which they were attached, was made of wood. The ploughs were very heavy and were often set on wheels and drawn by a team of oxen.

How to make the plough

Materials: sticks, wood, cardboard, 2 circular box lids, balsa cement, scissors, craft knife, paint, brush

Find some dry sticks about 1cm thick. Cut lengths 18cm and 30cm for wheel axle and main beam, and a forked piece 17cm high for handle. Strip off bark.

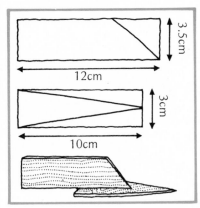

Carve share and mouldboard from thin pieces of fruit-box wood. Glue share under mouldboard. Use balsa cement for gluing all wooden parts.

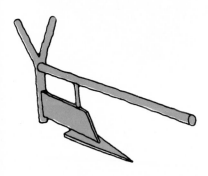

Glue mouldboard and main beam to handle. Use a small wooden support between main beam and mouldboard.

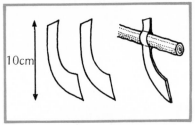

Cut 2 cardboard pieces for coulter. Glue together around main beam.

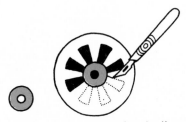

Cut 2 cardboard circles 4cm in diameter. Glue to centres of circular lids. Cut out sections for spokes.

Cover rims of wheels with strips of cardboard 1.5cm wide.

Fit wheels onto axle and glue in place.

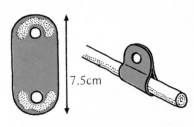

Cut piece of cardboard to connect beam to axle. Glue around axle.

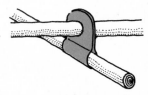

Push main beam through hole in cardboard. Glue it in place.

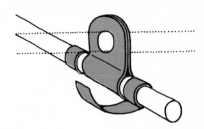

Wind small strips of card around axle on each side of centre piece to prevent main beam slipping.

Paint wheels of plough to look like wood, and coulter to look like iron.

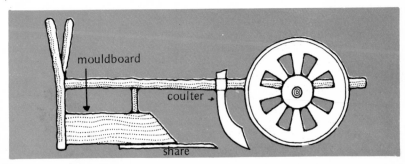

ISLAMIC MINARETS

The religion called Islam was founded by Muhammed the Prophet, who lived in Arabia from A.D. 570 to 632. The followers of Islam are Muslims, and the buildings in which they worship are called mosques.

The main part of the mosque is the large domed hall. The towers around the mosque are minarets. Minarets vary in size and design, but most are slender and cylindrical with tapering spires. Some have beautifully proportioned bulbous shapes near the top, and some are decorated with coloured tiles. All minarets have at least one balcony, which is usually reached by an inside staircase. Five times each day the muezzin, the man whose duty it is to summon the faithful, climbs to the balcony. Facing the four points of the compass in turn, he gives the call to prayer: "Come to prayer. Come to salvation. There is no god but Allah."

How to make the minaret

Materials: 2 cardboard boxes, 2 matchboxes, cardboard tube, paper, scissors, ruler, glue, compasses, pencil, paint, paintbrush

Make 4 small balconies for rectangular box that forms minaret base. Cut insides of 2 matchboxes in half and glue 1 on each side of box.

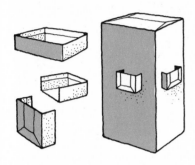

Measure tops of 2 boxes that form base and middle sections of minaret. On a piece of cardboard draw 2 rectangles 6cm longer and 6cm wider than tops.

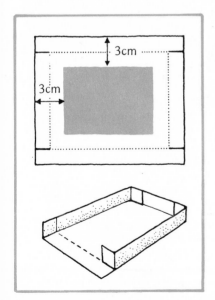

Cut out rectangles, crease and fold them to make two main balconies.

Cut 2 lengths of card 2.5cm wide for balcony railings. Cut slits into card and cut away alternate pieces. Glue railings onto inside edges of balconies.

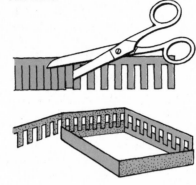

Make paper cone for cylindrical top of minaret. Cut ¼ section of a circle with radius 1½ times height of tube.

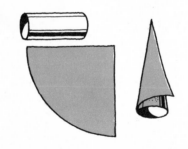

Curl paper into cone shape. Glue edges and glue onto tube.

Paint the 3 sections white and balconies and tube turquoise blue. Make windows, zig-zag patterns and all other decoration brown and grey.

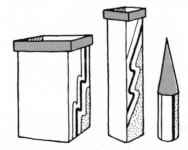

Glue balconies onto tops of boxes. Glue all sections together.

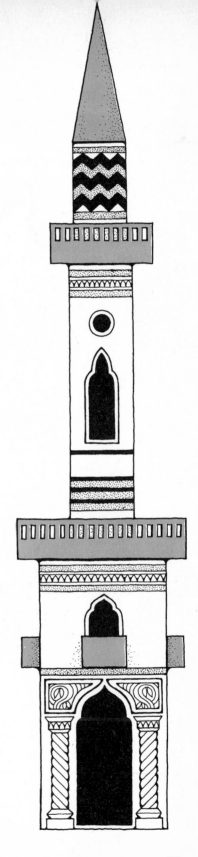

ROYAL CROWNS

During the Dark Ages kings in many parts of Europe became increasingly powerful. Only a few of the crowns used at their coronations remain. One Lombard crown was a ring of iron encrusted with jewels. Other crowns were made of iron plated with gold leaf. The gold plated crowns were usually decorated with precious gems brought to Europe from the East by traders.

The finest crown made during the Dark Ages is the magnificent 10th century crown in the Vienna Museum. It is made of pure gold. Four beautifully designed enamel plaques are set into the gold. The rest of the surface is completely covered with rubies, sapphires and emeralds. The raised arch stretching across the crown is made of gold into which pearls have been set. Dominating the front of the crown is a jewelled cross.

How to make the crown

Materials: cardboard, paper clip, dried peas or beads, pencil, ruler, compasses, scissors, glue, paints paintbrush

Cut piece of cardboard long enough to fit round your head. On it draw crown shape of 6 squares, 2 rectangles, and tab at one end.

Round top of each section using compasses or circular object like a tin. Draw cross on front section and tab on last section.

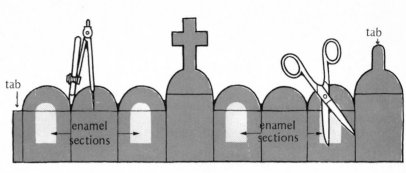

Crease along lines between sections. Bend crown into shape and secure temporarily with paper clip.

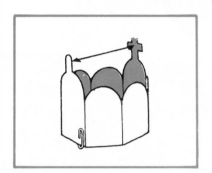

Measure diameter of crown for arch section. Draw arch piece on cardboard and cut out.

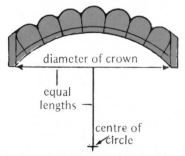

Paint crown and arch gold, and colour small enamel sections. To assemble crown, glue tab on first section behind rectangular back section. Glue arch between cross and tab on top of back section.

Decorate the crown with jewels. Glue on plastic beads, buttons, dried peas or beans painted bright colours.

First published in Great Britain 1978 by Owlet Books, Mills & Boon
Limited, 17–19 Foley Street, London W1A 1DR.

Owlet Books
© Mills & Boon Ltd 1978

THE DARK AGES   ISBN 0 263 06337 2

Printed in Italy